Squeaks and Cheeps

What You See and Hear in Animal Homes

By Marla Tomlinson

Discover Plants and Animals
Vowel Teams
(ea, ee, ey)

NORWOOD HOUSE  PRESS

DEAR CAREGIVER, *The Decodables* series contains books following a systematic, cumulative phonics scope and sequence aligned with the science of reading. Each book allows its reader to apply their phonics knowledge in engaging and relatable texts. The words within each text have been carefully selected to ensure that readers can rely on their decoding skills as they encounter new or unfamiliar words. They also include high frequency words appropriate for the target skill level of the reader.

When reading these books with your child, encourage them to sound out words that are unfamiliar by attending to the target letter(s) and sounds. If the unknown word is an irregularly spelled high frequency word or a word containing a pattern that has yet to be taught (challenge words) you may encourage your child to attend to the known parts of the word and provide the pronunciation of the unknown part(s). Rereading the texts multiple times will allow your child the opportunity to build their reading fluency, a skill necessary for proficient comprehension.

You can be confident you are providing your child with opportunities to build their decoding abilities which will encourage their independence as they become lifelong readers.

Happy Reading!

Emily Nudds, M.S. Ed Literacy
Literacy Consultant

Norwood House Press • www.norwoodhousepress.com
The Decodables ©2024 by Norwood House Press. All Rights Reserved.
Printed in the United States of America.
367N–082023

Library of Congress Cataloging-in-Publication Data has been filed and is available at https://lccn.loc.gov/2023010401

Literacy Consultant: Emily Nudds, M.S.Ed Literacy
Editorial and Production Development and Management: Focus Strategic Communications Inc.
Editors: Christine Gaba, Christi Davis-Martell
Photo Credits: Shutterstock: Adam Ke (p. 13), Alexey Seafarer (p. 20), Astrid Gast (p. 16), Betty Shelton (p. 7), colacat (p. 6), davidhoffmann photography (p. 14), Debbie Steinhausser (p. 8) francesco de marco (p. 16), GiGi Brock (p. 21), higrace (p. 17), Julian Wiskemann (p. 15), Kateryna_Moroz (p. 13), kosolovskyy (p. 11), Louise Ekeblad (p. 5), Macrovector (covers), Milan Zygmunt (p. 19), Oakland Images (p. 12), Paul Tymon (cover, p. 4), R J Endall Photographer (p. 18), Rodrigo Cuel (p. 10), SergeUWPhoto (p. 14), Shengyong Li (p. 19), Teo Tarras (p. 9), Tony Quinn (p. 6), Zadiraka Evgenii (p. 17).

Hardcover ISBN: 978-1-68450-691-0   Paperback ISBN: 978-1-68404-899-1
eBook ISBN: 978-1-68404-954-7

Contents

Habitats:
What's in a Home?

There are many things to see and hear in **habitats**. A habitat is where living things make their home. It has the right things to help that animal live.

You can see the breeze moving wheat in the field. You can hear the squeak of the mice who live there.

In a forest, you may meet a deer or hear the cheep of a bird.

Wheat fields are good homes for mice.

This polar bear is seeking its meal!

In a hot desert, you will see animals that like the heat. You may hear the screech of a hawk.

You can hear a polar bear smack the ice to find food in their cold **tundra** home.

There are many habitats. Some **key** ones are:
- Forest
- Grassland
- Wetland
- **Marine**
- Desert/Tundra
- Tropical Forests

Habitats are busy places full of life. They have all the things an animal needs to be safe and grow.

5

Forests:
In the Trees

What can you see and hear in a busy forest? Many animals call it home. You have the small chipmunks who like to live alone in holes. You can hear them rush around the forest as they get nuts to eat.

You can hear birds tweet. You can see them fly and weave through the trees. Many birds live in forest trees.

This chipmunk stuffs nuts into its cheek.

Blue jays live in forests across North America.

Deer can leap at least 6 feet in the air.

If you go for a hike in the woods, you could see a deer. You may hear a scream. Don't fear! It's just a yell of the fox. They sleep in a house called a **den** and play in the leaves.

Deep in the woods you may greet a bear. It can make a log creak when it seeks a meal. Bears eat a lot of different foods. It may feed on fish from a stream or some berries from a bush.

This fox has made a den in a tree.

Tropical Forests:
In the Heat and Rain

Many places around the globe have forests. Some are alike and others are very different.

A **tropical** rainforest is a **lush** and green forest found in places with a lot of heat. It rains most of the year. Rainforest trees are very tall. They all want sun so they reach high in the sky.

The rainforest is thick with trees and plants.

A toucan is quite the sight! This bird has a bright beak and makes its home in the trees of the rainforest. They eat fruit. This helps the trees and plants grow because they drop the seeds on the ground. This makes more fruit trees grow.

FUN FACT

Toucans can fly but like to hop around.

Toucans use their beak to peel fruit.

Grasslands:
In the Weeds

Grasslands are wide areas of grass, flowers, and weeds. Many bugs and animals call grasslands home.

Mice will feast on beans and peas. You can hear them squeak as they eat. Bees can be seen in flowers. They buzz as they seek food.

Bees like grasslands with their many flowers.

Grasslands are a great home for grasshoppers! These bugs can leap about 30 inches. That's a lot when they are only 2 inches in size.

The one sound you can hear from a grasshopper is like a snap or buzz. They make this sound by rubbing their legs against their wings.

Grasshoppers can feast on leaves in grasslands.

Marine:
In and Near the Water

By the ocean, you can see the water **gleam**. The sun seems to shine off it.

There is water all over the world and there are many different habitats in these waters. Some habitats are in the **shallow** water. Sea stars or clams live there.

A coral reef is often found in warm and shallow water. It is home to many **breeds** of fish and other marine life.

FUN FACT

There are more fish in the Atlantic Ocean than we have people on Earth!

This yellow tang fish is one of over 7,000 kinds of life seen in coral reefs.

Sea stars are found in many areas of the ocean, from shallow to deep water.

Then there are deep water habitats. Sharks and whales call the deeper water home.

In the ocean, you may see a whale leap out of the water. This is called a breach.

You may see a big group of fish. This is called a school. A school helps keep them safe.

A school of fish is neat to see.

This whale shows how high it can breach.

The beach is a busy habitat. Many animals live on beaches or other areas near the water.

Sea turtles hatch from their eggs on beaches. Then they need to go to the water. They can be seen around the world.

These baby sea turtles make their way to the water.

Seals sleep on the sand or rocks in a big heap. They like the warm sun. Then they take a swim in the **teal** sea.

There are also many birds to see on a beach. Seagulls and heron like to feed on fish and bugs.

You can hear seals bark when you go to an ocean.

This heron seeks a meal from the sea.

Wetlands: In Water and Weeds

Wetlands are places where the land is very wet or even covered in water. A lot of plants grow there. It is also home to many bugs and animals.

Ducks like wetlands because they eat bugs and water grass.

Ducks will put their head in the water to eat plants and bugs.

Wetlands may also be called a marsh, bog, or swamp.

Otters make a squeak-like sound.

There are a lot of reeds and other water grass in wetlands.

If you sneak a peek in the reeds, you may spot some otters as they play. Otters like all types of water. They live in wetlands, rivers, lakes, and creeks. You can even find some in the ocean.

Deserts:
In a Dry Home

A desert is a very dry area. It gets very little rain all year. There are not a lot of plants.

Many hot deserts have a lot of sand. Animals who live here need to be able to get or store water in different ways. Camels keep a lot of water in their body. This means they do not need to drink often.

Hot deserts are also home to many snakes and lizards.

This horned lizard likes the desert heat.

FUN FACT

Camels can go about 10 days without water!

Another kind of desert is a tundra. A tundra gets very little rain each year. It also does not have a lot of plants.

But a tundra is cold!

You can see fox and polar bears in a tundra. You can hear the seals bark and the snowy owl hoot.

You can see this sleek fox in a tundra habitat.

There is a lot for you to see and hear in animal habitats. The key is to wait and be quiet like a mouse. Don't leap about like a monkey!

You must be quiet to sneak a clean peek at a rabbit before it hops away.

Glossary

breeds: different types of an animal

den: an animal home that can be underground or built by the animal

gleam: to shine

habitats (hăb- ə-tăts): places where animals live

key: main part

lush: thick, full, and healthy

marine (mə-rēn): in or around water

shallow (shăl-ō): not deep

teal: a blue and green color

tropical (trŏ-pĭ-kəl): hot and wet area

tundra (tŭn-drə): a cold, dry area with little plant life and no trees

Index

Vowel Teams

ea			ee			ey
beach	heat	sea	bees	green	seeds	key
beak	leap	seals	breeds	greet	seek	monkey
beans	least	sneak	breeze	keep	seems	
clean	leaves	squeak	cheek	meet	seen	
creak	meal	stream	cheep	need	sleek	
fear	near	teal	creeks	peek	sleep	
feast	neat	weave	deep	peel	tree	
gleam	peas	wheat	deer	reeds	tweet	
heap	reach	year	feed	screech	weeds	
hear	scream		feet	see		

High-Frequency Words

air	around	different	good	live	over	through
also	away	does	great	most	play	very
animal	because	even	house	off	shows	want
another	before	found	little	only	small	year

Challenging Words

against	bright	Earth	grow	ocean	shallow	sound
bear	busy	fly	hawk	polar	sharks	turtles
berries	call	fruit	hoot	school	sight	warm
birds	could	group	mouse			